Original title:
Currents of Life's Story

Copyright © 2025 Creative Arts Management OÜ
All rights reserved.

Author: Tobias Winslow
ISBN HARDBACK: 978-1-80587-441-6
ISBN PAPERBACK: 978-1-80587-911-4

Seasons in Motion

Spring sneezed and made it rain,
Summer's sun did wax and wane,
Autumn danced with leaves in tow,
Winter's chill made snowmen grow.

Time hops like a rabbit mad,
With seasonal madness making us glad,
Days blend like yogurt and jam,
Each tick a new goofy slam.

The Weaving of Fate

Life's a tapestry so wide,
With threads pulled by chance and pride,
Stitches made with laughter's thread,
And a few that slipped away instead.

The loom's a-jump with hiccuped twists,
Running along with tangled lists,
Patterns shift as we all weave,
Quirks emerge with every leave.

Reflections on the Surface

Puddles mirror a jester's face,
Bubbles float with giggles in space,
Ripples carry jokes around,
While fish roll their eyes with a sound.

Laughter cracks like ice on a pond,
Making us question what's beyond,
What's splashed above and what's below,
A riddle danced with a cheeky flow.

Splashes of Color

Paint drips from a brush with flair,
Creating chaos, bright and rare,
A rainbow sneezed, it went awry,
Colors mixed, oh my, oh my!

Dancing hues on a canvas stretch,
An artist's palette starts to fetch,
The laughter echoes, shades unite,
In a wacky world of pure delight.

Cascading Journeys

In a river of socks without a mate,
I paddle my boat, still looking for fate.
Fish sing with glee, throwing me a wink,
As I trip on my laces and spill my drink.

Rides in a purse, where coins collide,
A wallet with secrets that giggle and hide.
I chase after dreams that float like a kite,
While a cat eyes my sandwich, as it takes flight.

The Undercurrents of Time

Time's like a waiter with wobbly hands,
Serving reminders, but no time to stand.
I spill my tea, it dances like jazz,
While a clock grins wide, 'Hey, time's just a faze!'

Tick-tock, tick-tock, the moments parade,
While I fumble my lines, like a grand charade.
Life's just a stage, with a laugh and a spin,
And I'm the clown with spaghetti for skin!

Ripples of Experience

Jumping in puddles, I'm splashed by a laugh,
Oh look, a duck with a floating giraffe!
I paddle through memories that giggle and squirm,
While the sun plays hide and seek, letting me burn.

Each quack a reminder, each splash a surprise,
As I navigate chaos with marshmallow eyes.
Life's recipe's funny, with sprinkles on top,
And I'm baking laughter while trying to hop!

The Journey Beneath

Under the surface where tickles reside,
Swims a fish wearing glasses, oh what a ride!
He flips and he flops, with a wink and a cheer,
As I trip on my joy, spilling giggles, oh dear!

The treasures we find, in laughter and jest,
Are scattered like breadcrumbs, a comedic quest.
So I'll swim through this farce, with a smile so wide,
For the journey's absurd, oh where will it slide?

Glimpses of the Unknown

In a field of socks I wonder,
Which ones might be paired under?
A story spinning, quite absurd,
With every mismatched little bird.

I tripped on dreams, and socks as well,
They whispered secrets, yet they fell.
Around the corner, laughter rolled,
As life unfolds, the tales retold.

A Flowing Narrative

Tea spills a tale of morning glories,
While buttered toast recalls its stories.
The cat insists upon the cheese,
A life of crumbs, with purrs to please.

As butter melts, the clock ticks by,
Each second winks, it's all a lie.
With every sip, my thoughts do dance,
A flowing lens, a silly chance.

The Ocean of Experiences

In the ocean's wave, I lose my hat,
A seagull dons it, oh what a brat!
With every splash, a laughter's crest,
Life's a joke, but oh, it's the best.

Floating on dreams like jellyfish,
Wishing for more than just a dish.
But fishy tales swim deep and wide,
In salty humor, we reside.

Thoughts Floating by

My mind's a kite, it soars and dips,
Chasing clouds, and playful quips.
It dodges trees with zeal and flair,
While squirrels jest, without a care.

Thoughts like balloons with faces bright,
Drift away on a breezy flight.
They pop with giggles, then they're gone,
Life's a riddle, come, tag along!

The Map of Moments

Each hiccup on my map, a twist,
Like socks that vanish in the mist.
I stumble upon a smiling tree,
It laughs when I trip and spill my tea.

With every laugh, a mile I roam,
Finding treasures in my foam.
A compass mad, it spins in glee,
Leading me to a cat's tea spree.

I chase the winds, a kite in flight,
Dance with clouds, feel pure delight.
A map that bends, with jokes to share,
Adventure's sketch, a giggly dare.

Lighthouses of Reflection

In the mirror, a lighthouse stands,
Waving back with funny hands.
I trip and stumble, shadowy glance,
It cracks a smile, a goofy dance.

Shining bright with silly rays,
Guiding me through clumsy days.
Reflections chuckle, waves of cheer,
As I try to steer my career.

The lighthouse beams, a cosmic prank,
Launching boats from a rainbow tank.
In the seas of thought, I sail to land,
With giggles as my compass, unplanned.

The Voyage Continues

A ship of dreams on jelly waves,
Wobbles on while laughter braves.
With goofy sails and polka dots,
We navigate through silly spots.

The captain's got a nose like cheese,
Charting routes with giggles and wheeze.
Each wave a chuckle, splash, and roar,
As fish wear hats and dance on shore.

Through storms of giggles, off we glide,
With candy skies and laughter as our guide.
The voyage hums a funny tune,
A charming song beneath the moon.

Pebbles in the Stream

I tossed a pebble, seen it bounce,
It landed near a dancing mouse.
We shared a laugh as ripples spread,
A concert of giggles, a jelly bread.

The stream flows on with playful glee,
Tickling stones and a wobbly bee.
Each splash a note in nature's song,
With every turn, nothing feels wrong.

As pebbles skip, I'm led to play,
In sunny spots where shadows sway.
The stream whispers secrets of delight,
In reflections of humor, bright as light.

Rhythms of Reflection

In the mirror, I dance a jig,
My reflection laughs, oh so big.
With every twist and silly spin,
Life's a party, let's begin!

Mirror, mirror, who's the best?
Is it me in this sparkly vest?
A wink and nod, a cheeky grin,
Here's a show where all can win!

If trees could laugh, they'd shake with glee,
At squirrels who think they're acrobats, you see!
Nature's stage is quite the treat,
With whispered jokes and a winged beat.

So let's reflect, with glee not dread,
Life's a circus; wear a funny hat instead!
With laughter ringing, we won't rue,
For jesters rule when skies are blue!

Waves of Transformation

A wave rolled in, with frothy flair,
Tangled hair, no time to care.
I surfed the tide on a backyard slide,
With rubber ducks right by my side!

The seafoam tickled, oh what fun,
Splashing about, we're not yet done!
A leap, a splash, my phone took flight,
Goodbye selfies, hello delight!

Fish in the sea swim past with grace,
While I flounder in this weird place.
Yet every flop is laughter's song,
In this big splash, we all belong!

So ride the waves, don't be a bore,
With giggles echoing to the shore.
In every twist of fortune's hand,
We find the joy, as life's unplanned!

The Ebb and Flow of Dreams

In my dreams, I take a flight,
Over fields, oh what a sight!
I wore pajamas, no shoes in sight,
Sailing through clouds, feeling light!

A fish in a tux, quite debonair,
Sang me songs without a care.
"Don't forget to wear a tie!"
I laughed so hard, I nearly cried.

Magic carpets zoom and zip,
While I turn and do a flip.
With aliens playing hopscotch too,
Who knew the night could be this kooky crew?

So in the ebb, in the flow,
Dreams take us where whimsy goes.
With laughter bright as morning beams,
Life's a game; don't crush your dreams!

A Canvas of Change

With paintbrushes and colors bright,
I throw my art into the night.
A splash of blue, a dash of green,
A masterpiece that's quite obscene!

Swirls and twirls, oh what a sight,
I painted my cat as Captain White!
With polka-dots and silly hats,
He sits enthroned with all the bats.

Splattering joy, a lovely mess,
Every color's my wild guess.
Changing hues with every stroke,
My canvas giggles; it's no joke!

So dance around with brush in hand,
Create the wackiest, wildest brand.
For life's a palette, bold and strange,
Let laughter lead, embrace the change!

Tides of Time

Time tickles like a feather,
As it dances through the air.
Got lost on my way to adulthood,
But hey, I'm still learning, I swear.

Socks on my hands, I shuffle,
Pretending I'm a fancy clown.
While life throws pies of laughter,
I just try not to fall down.

Chasing dreams in oversized shoes,
Bumbling with glee through the mess.
The clocks laugh loud, they refuse,
To take me serious, I confess.

Every wrinkle tells a tale,
Of stumbles that make us grin.
Life's a joke on a grand scale,
And humor is where we begin.

Whispers of Tomorrow

Tomorrow waves like a flag,
With promises and a wink.
I trip over coffee mugs,
As if they're plotting, I think.

I plan to be a great success,
But first, I'll finish this snack.
Life gives me riddles to guess,
As I keep each pizza on track.

The birds chirp silly secrets,
While squirrels dance in delight.
I'll chase dreams in mismatched socks,
Maybe I'll sleep through the night.

Jokes invade my mind like bees,
Buzzing with thoughts oh so bright.
Each whisper hints at a breeze,
That blows my worries from sight.

Unraveled Threads

Life's a knitting project gone wild,
A scarf with colors so bright.
With each loop, I'm a confused child,
Pulling yarn with giddy delight.

Unraveled threads around my feet,
Like life's surprises in store.
I trip and giggle on this street,
Who said that I'd keep it in lore?

Each stitch a story I weave,
Of laughter, tears, and mishaps.
I look at the mess I conceive,
And think, "I'll just call it all apps."

The fabric of days can fray,
But I'll wrap it in a grin.
For every twist shows me the way,
And fun is where all starts to spin!

Ebb and Flow

Waves crash with a tickle here,
While I build castles of dreams.
They wash away, but that's quite clear,
Life's more fun than it seems.

I chase the tide, a playful breeze,
And stumble in the wet sand.
Why take it serious, if you please?
Falling's part of the plan, so grand!

The moon winks at my silly stance,
As the ocean foams and giggles.
Each wave invites me to dance,
With all its zany wiggles.

In this tidal play I thrive,
Forget the serious and strife.
In every ebb, a laugh will drive,
And make a joke of this life!

Within the Flow

In a river of socks lost, oh so sly,
They float like boats, just passing by.
Caught in a whirlpool of mismatched pairs,
Life laughs at us, it doesn't care.

Bubbles of laughter, we tumble and spin,
Chasing the giggles, where do we begin?
Rafts made of dreams, on puddles we glide,
In this splishy-splashy, goofy wild ride.

Merging with Time

Tick-tock the clock, it's a game of charades,
Time wriggles and jigs, in funny cascades.
It trips on its laces, a clown in the night,
While seconds keep slipping, oh what a sight!

Seconds like fish, they dart all around,
While minutes wear hats, and joy has been found.
With laughter as bait, we cast out our lines,
Life's a big party, with dance and with rhymes.

Stories Beneath the Waves

Under the sea, where the fish like to plot,
They gather for gossip, oh what a lot!
With seaweed for wigs and a coral tiara,
Their tales are just endless, like a wild opera!

Whales hum a tune, but it's out of sync,
They giggle and splash, creating a wink.
Fishes tap dance on shells, such a scene,
Under the waves, life's a comedy routine.

Sustaining the Journey

With backpacks of snacks, we're ready to roam,
Each step is a stomp, we're far from our home.
Quirky companions, we're all out of tune,
But laughter is plenty, we'll sing to the moon.

The hills may be steep, and the paths may be long,
But we'll trot along, singing our song.
With marshmallows toasted and stories to tell,
Our silly adventures, they suit us so well.

A Journey of Whispers

In the stream where ducks do waddle,
I lost my shoe, it's not aaddle.
Fish are laughing, what a spree,
Who knew my float was just a tree!

I tossed a line, caught a shoe,
The fish all said, 'Hey, how do you do?'
With every splash, my sense of pride,
Floated right away, like a fishy ride!

I sung a tune, off-key, of course,
A frog croaked back, "What's your remorse?"
The bubbles giggled, danced in glee,
While turtles joined, as merry as can be!

Finally home, with tales to spill,
Of what I saw by the little hill.
A shoe, a frog, and laughter galore,
Next time I'll remember, shoes aren't for oar!

Secrets in the Stream

In a brook where whispers play,
I dropped my sandwich, what a day!
A squirrel peeked with a cheeky grin,
"Did you want a snack?" he asked with sin.

The water danced, a giggly tease,
While minnows swirled with utmost ease.
They planned a party—who brought the cake?
Oh wait, it's lunch, for goodness' sake!

A sneaky otter stole my hat,
I tried to chase, but fell—how 'bout that?
The fish all laughed, threw a water bomb,
At this rate, I'll just fish for calm!

Under the bridge, they share their tales,
Of bubble baths and wind-blown sails.
I'll return, swim with my dream,
And maybe snag a fish with cream!

The Water's Embrace

The river called, with a bubbly shout,
"Jump right in, there's fun about!"
But I slipped hard, landed with a splash,
Even the frogs said, "Now, that was brash!"

As waters swirled, they started to sing,
"Welcome back to the splashes and bling!"
The fish wore hats, the turtles danced,
Life's a party when you take a chance!

"Watch your toes!" a fish proclaimed,
While dodging rocks, I felt so ashamed.
The current spilled my secrets loud,
Now I'm the joke of the river crowd!

But laughter echoed, sweet and clear,
No one cared about my fear.
So here's to the slips and splashes I make,
In the water's embrace, all's fair game at stake!

Sailing Through Shadows

With a banana for a boat, I set sail,
Through shadows where the fish all pale.
The sunbeam giggled, "What's your plight?"
"Can't steer this thing, it's outta sight!"

Clouds shaped like ducks flew overhead,
I waved back, though they might be dead.
A turtle cried, "You're looking lost!"
"Just navigating," I puffed at great cost!

Suddenly, a wave flipped me round,
And I learned just why ducks don't drown.
I splashed and spun, like a whirlpool's dance,
While ducks all cheered for my clumsy chance!

Now I'm a captain of absurd delight,
In shadows where giggles steal the night.
So if you see my banana boat,
Just wave hello; I'm afloat, not remote!

The Pathways of Reflection

Wander down the winding road,
Where squirrels play their acorn load.
Each step a dance, a laughing spring,
While birds debate the songs to sing.

Puddles mirror faces bright,
Making frowns a pure delight.
I trip on thoughts that come and go,
Chasing cats who steal the show.

The trees gossip in a rustling breeze,
While ants march past with cheeky ease.
Life's a jest, a quirky twist,
A punchline waiting to be kissed.

So giggle loud and tread with care,
In the paths where jokes are rare.
For every laugh, a memory grows,
In this grand play, everyone knows!

Beneath the Waters

A fish in socks, it swims so gay,
With bubbles that swirl in a comedic way.
Octopus jokes at the coral bar,
While crabs play cards near a passing star.

The seaweed dances to a whale's cool tune,
As jellyfish float with a silly swoon.
Fish avoiding the bait, oh what a sight,
Life's an ocean of giggles, pure delight.

A treasure chest filled with tales untold,
Of sea cucumbers that thought they were bold.
Dolphins snicker, pulling pranks on the ships,
As mermaids dive into laughter's sweet dips.

So let's dive deep, in blue so bright,
Where laughter bubbles and fish take flight.
Hold your breath, let's have a ball,
For under the waves, we all stand tall!

The Drift of Time

Tick-tock goes the clock so sly,
While socks disappear, oh my, oh my!
Time flies past on roller skates,
Rushing like it can't wait for dates.

A cheesy grin on a snail's slow track,
Counting minutes as it's never slack.
The sun plays tricks, a game of peek,
While moonlight giggles, it's never meek.

Forget the race, let's ride the waves,
With laughter that bubbles and mischief that saves.
For in each tick, there lies a jest,
A wacky whirl of time that's best.

So spin and twirl, embrace the flight,
For each moment has its own delight.
Laughter and time, a wondrous rhyme,
In the grand dance where all is prime!

Reflections in Motion

Mirrors giggle as we pass by,
Making faces, oh the sly!
Down the hall, a dancing tune,
While shadows shimmy into the noon.

Laughter echoes through the glass,
Time skips along, watch it pass.
Water droplets race and play,
In the laughter of the day.

Kids leap high, try to touch the sun,
While clouds chuckle, just for fun.
Reflections twist, a silly sight,
In the dance of day and night.

So spin and sway, don't mind the flaws,
For life's a mirror of giggles and paws.
In this reflection, find your bliss,
For each moment's a silly kiss!

Whispers of the Past

Old socks in the drawer, what a sight,
Reminding me of days that felt just right.
They bear the tales of clumsy mischief,
A secret dance, an old sock's wish.

Grandma's tales of love and lore,
Yet each time I hear them, I snore.
Her knitting needles, clickity-clack,
Spinning yarn like a mental snack.

A cat with swagger, a mischievous glare,
Chasing dust bunnies without a care.
The clock on the wall ticks loud and slow,
As memories swirl in a funny flow.

So here's to the past with all its quirks,
Where goofy moments and laughter lurks.
With socks and stories, we smile and sigh,
Painting our lives with a wink and a pie.

Navigating the Unknown

A GPS that leads to a fancied place,
But instead, it hops on a freeway race.
Turn left, turn right, or go round and round,
Who knew a wrong turn could bring such sound?

Adventurous spirits, on this ride we opt,
Where snacks fly around and soda's flopped.
We vow it's a journey, not just a race,
With laughter and crumbs smeared on our face.

A squirrel with dreams, a tree top dancer,
Mocking our path like a silly romancer.
We follow the signs but lose all the maps,
With giggles and jests, we plan our mishaps.

So here's to the unknown, our playful quest,
With goofy detours, we simply jest.
Life's a mixed bag, let's roll with delight,
Navigating confusion, we'll manage just right.

Streams of Change

He woke up thinking he'd wear a shoe,
Last week's fashion, something brand new.
But when he stepped out, oh what a sight,
His feet were screaming, 'This just ain't right!'

With each passing day, the style shifts fast,
Harem pants today, tomorrow they're past.
A shirt that sparkles, or just a plain tee,
In this stream of change, we just let it be.

Haircuts that shock like a lightning flash,
One day a wizard, the next a mustache.
With laughter around, we dip and we dive,
In this whirlpool of fun, we feel so alive.

So let's ride the waves, with humor in hand,
Skipping through changes, as life's unplanned.
Laughter our compass, in every new phase,
Savoring the silly, in all the new ways.

Footprints on the Water

A stroll on the beach with shoes in hand,
Left prints on the shore, but what a strand!
They danced with the waves, then slipped away,
Leaving me laughing, like a game we play.

Wet sand squishes, like a ticklish tease,
With each silly step, I wobbled with ease.
My friends roll their eyes, but I just can't stop,
As I slip and I slide—oh! Watch out for the plop!

Where water meets land, confusion's a blast,
Every wave kisses footprints, then they're outclassed.
With laughter and splashes and the sea breeze delight,
Footprints on water, a whimsical sight.

So if you find joy where the puddles form,
Dance like nobody's watching, just weather the storm.
In the tides of our lives, we wade and we play,
Leaving footprints on water, come what may!

A Symphony of Flows

A fish in a hat sings a tune,
While ducks in a line march by at noon.
The water's a stage for all to see,
With bubbles and splashes, it's quite a spree.

A frog in a tux does a little jig,
While turtles compete in a slow-motion gig.
The reeds sway along, adding to the song,
In this wacky ballet, nothing feels wrong.

The otters debate who is the best,
While minnows plan their own little fest.
And crabs clap their claws in perfect time,
Creating a rhythm that's simply sublime.

With laughter and joy, the currents do flow,
In this zany dance where silly things grow.
Every ripple a laugh, every splash a cheer,
In this symphony of flows, we find good cheer.

Navigating the Waters of Time

A boat with a cat sails too much beer,
While a wise old fish gives tips from the rear.
The waves seem to giggle as they roll along,
As seagulls compose a slightly off-key song.

Drifting along, we bump into boats,
With raccoons in tuxedos, draped in fine coats.
They sip on their drinks, with a wink and a grin,
As the boat spins around, and we all join in.

A coconut floats, wearing sunglasses bright,
While jellyfish dance in the moon's silver light.
The sailors take turns telling tales of the sea,
Each one more wild than the last, oh me!

Through whirlpools of laughter and waves of delight,
We navigate waters, both day and night.
With fun as our compass, we never will tire,
Charting our course with a giggle and mire.

The Stream's Embrace

In a stream where the critters all gather to play,
A squirrel wears goggles and shoots for the spray.
Beavers are wrestling, what a sight to behold,
While otters crack jokes that never get old.

A turtle in cargo shorts splashes about,
While minnows throw parties and swim all out.
The pebbles are bouncing in snickers and cheer,
As the water flows by with its giggly sneer.

A duck leads the line like a captain so grand,
With a squeaky-toy voice, taking charge of the band.
Their harmony echoes through the trees up high,
While frogs join in chorus with "ribbit" and sigh.

In the stream's sweet embrace, joy dances so bright,
With laughter and bubbles, it feels just right.
Each twist and each turn, a merry escape,
In this watery world where fun takes shape.

A Journey of Echoes

Echoes of laughter bounce off the shore,
As crabs tell tales of the waves they swore.
A pelican pirouettes on a soapbox high,
While jellybeans float by, oh my, oh my!

The otters compete in a race with a snail,
While frogs leap in sync, making quite the trail.
With giggles and splashes, the fun takes its turn,
As the sun dips low and the fireflies learn.

A raccoon wears sneakers and chases a dream,
While fish form a choir and compile a theme.
Each echo a chuckle, each wave makes a sound,
In this quirky journey, pure joy can be found.

The moon grins down on this whimsical show,
Where all creatures gather to play and to flow.
With smiles and joy, we share this delight,
In the echoes of laughter, everything's right.

Echoes of the Past

Once I tripped on my own two feet,
And danced like a goose to a jazz beat.
My childhood tales, they're quite a mess,
With socks on my hands, I played dress!

The cat thought it was a grand parade,
While I wore my mom's shoes, I felt so spayed.
Each tumble I took, a laugh in the air,
But let's not discuss the time with the chair.

Grandpa's stories, wild and tall,
Involving aliens and a bouncy ball.
He swears he's seen some crazy sights,
Like puppies in spaceships flying kites!

So here I stand, a jester in rhyme,
Turning my past into comedic time.
With each funny tale, a chuckle's released,
For laughter, dear friends, is the best feast!

Silent Streams

In the park where the kiddies play,
I lost my sandwich, oh what a day!
A squirrel thought it was his fine buffet,
He took it and dashed, now that's just gray!

A splash in the water, a (not so) swift dive,
My shoes got soaked, but I felt so alive.
The ducks quacked loudly, gave me a stare,
As I awkwardly flailed, splashing everywhere!

In puddles I leapt, a joyful ballet,
While onlookers watched with no words to say.
Life's quiet streams, a riotous dance,
In my world of mayhem, I'll take every chance!

I may not be graceful, but oh what a show,
Every slip and a slide, a chance for a glow.
With hidden giggles and chuckles anew,
In this flowing tale, it's the joy we imbue!

The Dance of Winds

The wind blew my hat, off it flew high,
Chasing it down with a gleeful sigh.
It landed on someone's dog, oh dear,
That pup looked so regal, it was quite clear!

I waved and apologized, feeling quite spry,
But the dog just danced, a true four-legged guy.
He pranced on the grass, my hat on his head,
Making me giggle, let's just not tread!

Balloons in the air, a colorful sight,
I tried to catch one, but lost my height.
I soared like a kite, with a laugh and a spin,
Only to land with a giant grin!

So here's to the winds, guiding our fate,
Whirling and twirling, oh life is quite great.
With giggles and hats in delightful dismay,
Let's dance with the breezes, come what may!

Facets of Fate

The fortune teller said I'd find gold,
But all I discovered were socks threefold.
Each left on a journey, where could they be?
In the land of mismatched, oh woe is me!

At dinner, I spilled sauce all over my shirt,
Claimed it was art, my outfit's expert.
The spaghetti danced, in a splashy finale,
While my family giggled, a dinner party rally.

I tried to impress with a magic trick,
But my wand was a broom, now that's quite slick!
I ended up sweeping, the crowd was amazed,
With laughter and broomsticks, my heart was ablaze!

So fate may toss twists, like leaves in the breeze,
I'll take every fumble with giggles and ease.
For in this grand tale, a smile's the reward,
With silly surprises, the best of the hoard!

Ripples of Existence

In the pond, a frog does leap,
Creating ripples, secrets to keep.
A napkin sails, on a picnic scene,
How messy can peanut butter mean?

Squirrels plot their heist with flair,
A stolen acorn, they think is fair.
Yet in my pocket, I find old fries,
Not quite a treasure, but a tasty surprise.

In life's tiny quirks we play and fumble,
With every slip, we laugh and tumble.
The cat strolls in, sits where it's hot,
While I ponder why I bought that pot.

Oh, the dance of everyday's delight,
With each misstep, the world feels right.
So let's splash about, make some noise,
And collect memories like toys for the boys.

Navigating the Unknown

In a maze of mismatched socks,
I sail through life, avoiding clocks.
"Where's the other?" I often sigh,
As my laundry monsters seem to fly.

With a compass made of crumbs and cheer,
I wander 'round, no end is near.
I follow the dog; he sniffs like a pro,
Finding lost tennis balls in the snow.

Through uncharted kitchens and forgotten pans,
I conquer stale bread and loose rubber bands.
With every "oops" and "what did I say?"
My maps seem drawn a bit wonky, I say.

Adventure awaits, tucked under my bed,
Where dust bunnies dance, and dreams are fed.
Join in the fun, hold laughter tight,
Navigating this chaos feels just right.

Waves of Memory

In the ocean of thoughts, we splash and play,
Surfers of time, we ride every wave.
A jellyfish stings, or so they say,
But in my world, it's just a ballet.

With each tide of laughter, we wash ashore,
Collecting seashells and jokes to store.
Grandma's tales of sandcastles high,
Turn into giggles that never say goodbye.

As the tide rolls back, they can't escape,
Those dolphins in tuxedos, what a shape!
They flip and flounder, creating a scene,
In my waves of memory, all things are keen.

I build a sandman, and he starts to melt,
Waving goodbye, oh, the joy I felt!
A splash here, a laugh there, life's silly song,
In waves of memory, we all belong.

Chasing the Horizon

Jogging on sand with mismatched shoes,
I chase the horizon, with nothing to lose.
A squirrel scoffs at my hurried pace,
"Why not stop and take a break?" he says with grace.

With a sandwich in hand and a bird in flight,
I ponder the chances of vegan delight.
The seagull squawks, my chance snack flies,
While I wave bye-bye with very sad eyes.

Stumbling upon a feast for ants,
I join their parade, in silly pants.
Together we celebrate life's random schemes,
A motley crew dancing in sunshine dreams.

Chasing the horizon, I trip with flair,
My feet tie-dyed in sun-kissed air.
In this crazy race, laughter leads the way,
And tomorrow awaits—a whole new play.

Sailing Through Shadows

The cat steals my lunch, oh what a sight,
A shadowy pirate in the kitchen light.
With paws on the counter, he claims every bite,
I sail my ship, but it's quite a fright.

The winds are a howl, my sails are in knots,
In a battle of wits, he claims all my spots.
The jellyfish dance, while the coffee still rots,
Am I captain or crew? Oh, I've got my thoughts!

Yet laughter abounds in this hungry duel,
His stealthy approach, a mischievous rule.
I navigate chaos, it's his witty school,
And in this wild storm, I just play the fool.

So here I float, on this creaky old boat,
With my feline first mate, always eager to gloat.
Life's messy adventures, they keep us afloat,
As I laugh with my mate, on this quirky old tote.

Embracing the Unknown

Woke up late, socks don't even match,
Danced with the mirror, oh what a catch!
In this wild whirlwind, there's always a hatch,
Embrace the absurd, it's quite the old batch.

Spilled all the cereal, the milk took a dive,
In this madcap kitchen, I try to survive.
With each wobbly step, my toes feel alive,
Who knew spoon-feeding chaos could be so contrive?

Riding the bus with a hat like a dream,
The fellow behind me lets out a loud scream.
Is life just a sitcom? Am I part of the scheme?
In this ballroom of laughter, I'm part of the team.

So here's to the mayhem, the whirls and the spins,
To the friends that I make and the laughter that wins.
With every mishap, the joy still begins,
In this game of surprises, true life's never thins.

Journeying Through the Frame

A picture on my wall just waved at me,
What a strange thought, am I losing my glee?
With frames of my past, they giggle with glee,
Each memory dances, like bees in a spree.

The old man in photos, he's juggled a cat,
While I'm stuck in traffic, a lizard as that.
In dreams, they all chatter, it's quite the format,
I join in their laughter, it's more than just chat.

With each click of my camera, I capture the jest,
A tree in a tutu, surely life's best.
The world's quite a stage, so come be my guest,
Get ready for antics, this life is a quest.

So journey with me, through this whimsical frame,
Let's ride on the wings of absurdity's fame.
Together we'll laugh, as we play silly games,
In this gallery of joy, we'll never feel shame.

The Boundless Odyssey

Set sail on a quest, a sandwich in hand,
With jelly all drippy, and my crew in demand.
We're off to find treasure—oh isn't it grand?
The map's just a doodle, but I still take a stand.

We dodge giant seagulls with their judgmental squawks,
As they steal my fries, oh, they really have guts!
My ship's built of laughter and wobbly blocks,
Adventure's our compass, and we steer with some guts!

Through waters of craziness, we sing off-key,
With dolphins that giggle, and waves that agree.
Each splash tells a tale, so wild and so free,
This odyssey's boundless, just you and me.

With each leap of faith, we greet the unknown,
Together we charge with silly undertones.
The universe chuckles as we drift and roam,
In this boundless journey, we've truly found home.

Stories in the Water

Splashing tales in the stream,
Fish with quirks, they often scheme.
Bubbles rise with every lie,
Giggling waves wave goodbye.

Drifting logs, they tell their jokes,
Whirling pools with dancing folks.
A turtle's wink, a duckling's dance,
Wet and wild, here's your chance!

Muddy shoes and soggy hats,
Cheeky frogs in all their spats.
Life's a splash, so take a dive,
In this pond, we all feel alive!

Waves can giggle, currents play,
Making fun of every day.
So when you wander by the brook,
Listen close, it's quite a book!

Mosaics of Memory

Pieces scattered, bright and bold,
Memories gleam like tales retold.
Laughter echoes, colors blend,
Funny moments, they won't end.

Coffee spills on the tablecloth,
A cat that ran, a sudden scoff.
Mismatched socks on toddler feet,
Every hue, a story sweet.

Tickling time with every glance,
Recollections in a dance.
Snippets crammed in jars of glass,
Chasing joy, let not it pass!

So grab a piece, let's make a start,
Crafting smiles, the perfect art.
In this collage of our days,
Funny memories in bright arrays!

The Language of Tides

Waves that whisper, tides that tease,
They speak secrets with such ease.
A seagull's squawk, a splashy sound,
Funny stories whirl around.

Crabs in coats, they wave their claws,
Out to lunch without a pause.
Paddle boards and beach ball fights,
Each tide brings fresh comic sights.

Surfboards wobble, folks take flight,
Grinning as they dash with might.
The ocean sings in silly rhymes,
Tickling toes, oh how it climbs!

So when you hear the water laugh,
Join the fun, go take a bath!
In the sea where memories glide,
Life's a jesting, joyous ride!

Chasing the Horizon

With sun hats on, we hit the road,
Chasing dreams, it's a funny code.
Clouds that float like marshmallow fluff,
While giggles bounce, we call that stuff.

The horizon grins, out of our reach,
But we'll outrun each sandy beach.
Laughter spills like a flashy kite,
In search of smiles, oh what a sight!

We tumble over unseen bumps,
Finding joy in every thump.
Winding paths with silly squeals,
Adventure calls, and laughter heals!

So pack your dreams, don't look back,
The vibe is fun on this crazy track.
Chasing the horizon, come take a ride,
With chuckles and joy, let's turn the tide!

The Flow of Tomorrow

In a river of socks, they float with glee,
Lost to the dryer, where could they be?
Fished out a sandwich, what a surprise,
A feast in the wash, do I hear cries?

Tomorrow will come with banana peels,
And ticklish thoughts from last night's meals.
Dance like a fish, flip and swirl,
Life's a swirl of giggles, watch it unfurl.

Next week's a maze of mismatched shoes,
Chasing the cat; I think I'll lose!
A comedy sketch in the hallway light,
Twisting in the joy, oh what a sight!

So here we go, on a wobbly ride,
Strapped in for laughs, come along for the glide.
With every turn, take a slice of pie,
Watch as the laughter dances, oh me, oh my!

Seamless Transitions

Slip on a shoe, but it's not quite right,
Stuck in two worlds, oh what a fright!
One's made of rubber, the other of foam,
I'm off to the park, but where is my home?

Juggling my thoughts like grapes in a bowl,
They bounce to the beat of my wobbly stroll.
Watch how they tumble, a colorful show,
Life's a circus; let the good times flow!

Coffee's a potion that warms up the day,
But spill it too fast, and it's chaos at play.
Frothing and bubbling like secrets unfold,
I'll wear it with pride, like a badge made of gold!

Transition is comical, funky, and fine,
Embrace every twist, let your quirks brightly shine.
So here's to the laughter, let's raise a cheer,
For the tangled up moments, we hold so dear!

The Passage of Moments

A clock on the wall ticks like a tune,
Lost in my thoughts, I'll be late for noon.
The cat's plotting schemes, a master of stealth,
While I'm in the fridge, raiding for wealth.

Moments pass by like ducks in a line,
Quacking and waddling, oh isn't it fine?
One's wearing boots, the other just socks,
In this parade, we're the playful clucks!

Forgetful grocery runs leave me in stitches,
Toaster's my friend; it makes crunchy riches.
I laugh at the chaos of forgotten plans,
As I whirl through my day like a dance of fans.

The moments, they wink, cheeky and sly,
Each tick of the clock is a reason to fly.
So sail with your humor, let madness ignite,
In this passage of giggles, our hearts are alight!

Shifts in the Tide

The ocean is giggling, it's pulling my leg,
Tide's in a tangle; where's the correct peg?
Seagulls are screeching, they're barefaced and bold,
Who knew salty air could turn you to gold?

I tried to build castles, but they melt and flow,
With sands on my sandwich, it's quite the show.
The waves are my canvas, and so I create,
A masterpiece of blunders, oh isn't it great?

Flip-flops are dancing their own quirky jig,
As I chase the retreating briny twig.
Underneath the sun, where all things collide,
Gaffes of delight shape the shifts in the tide.

So ride with the breeze, let the fun never cease,
Life's wild waves wash in with a tease.
With laughter as surf, and folly my guide,
I'll paddle through life, with glee as my stride!

Undercurrents of Thought

In the river of brains, thoughts swim all day,
Sometimes they bubble, other times they sway.
A fish wearing glasses with a deep little sigh,
Says, "I swear I saw noodles!" oh me, oh my!

That crabby old turtle with shoes on the sand,
Claims he once knitted a sweater, quite grand.
But sailors all chuckle and shout with delight,
As he walks in a circle, it's quite the strange sight.

A dolphin who dances, with flips in the air,
Wants to learn salsa, while folks just stare.
Says, "I'll swim in circles, so we won't go home,
Until my dance partner's a whiskered old gnome."

As thoughts drift and meander, like boats in the bay,
We laugh and we ponder, what thoughts went astray.
In the laughter of waves, like a joke shared with friends,
Who knew life would twist in such funny amends?

Beyond the Shore

On beaches of laughter where seagulls compete,
Sand's tickled by footprints and shells under feet.
A crab with a bucket and a beach ball to toss,
Says, "I'm the king!" with a cheeky little gloss.

The ocean wears glasses, though it's quite a feat,
To see the lost socks as it swallows up feet.
A whale in a top hat serves tea from a shell,
With crumpets and jelly, it all goes so well.

Shells gossip and chatter, it's all quite absurd,
One says "I once flew!" but it got overheard.
The others just laugh with a splash and a tease,
As fishes in tuxedos swim past with such ease.

Through waves that are giggling and frothy with cheer,
Life dances like bubbles that pop in the sphere.
Beyond all the sandcastles, laughter will soar,
As the tide tides away, we just want more and more!

Illumination of Moments

In the glow of the moon, a cat starts to sing,
With dreams of catching the stars on a string.
A raccoon in pajamas declares it's too bright,
As he stumbles for pizza, quite full of delight.

The fireflies waltz with their tiny little lights,
While frogs throw a party, oh what funny sights!
A squirrel dressed fancy, in a vest of pure gold,
Claims it's the best way to keep summer cold.

Moments like bubbles rise up in the air,
And pop with a chuckle, we giggle and stare.
The trees start to tickle our thoughts from above,
While owls tell jokes about the creatures they love.

In shimmers and glimmers of dusk that delight,
Time dances and spins in the warm twilight light.
Illumination glows with a wink and a grin,
For each fleeting moment is where we begin!

Mosaic of Experiences

In patches of laughter, we stitch and we thread,
Life's fabric unravels, then laughingly spread.
A butterfly whispers of broccoli days,
As squirrels hold classes on funny old ways.

With each sprinkle of colors, all wild and absurd,
Are tales spun like tales that we've all overheard.
Where llamas debate the best ways to prance,
And pigs in top hats find romance on a dance.

The tapestry shimmers in sunlight so clear,
As odd things entwine, we shout "Look over here!"
With a rhythm of giggles and hiccups we weave,
Our stories collide, and we never believe.

From moments of chaos to laughter-mixed cheers,
We cherish the fit of our mismatched careers.
In life's jumbled artwork, we find joy anew,
A mosaic of moments painted bright with a view!

Echoes in Time

I stepped on a leaf, it crunched with a sound,
A squirrel nearby fell from his mound.
He looked quite surprised, with a nut in his paws,
As if I'd broken some ancient laws.

The clock on the wall ticks a silly tune,
Time jumps like a frog beneath the full moon.
I chase after minutes like chasing a cat,
But it runs in circles, imagine that!

I tried to catch time in a jar made of glass,
It giggled and danced, then slipped right past.
Now it's floating around with my left shoe,
Oh, what a racket, a grand hullabaloo!

In the end, I learned, from the dust on my clock,
That laughter's the key to unlock every block.
So next time I trip over bright colored hue,
I'll just shout "surprise!" like a clown that's been true.

The Flow of Moments

In a world full of puddles, I jump and I slip,
I land in a fountain, oh, what a trip!
A fish gives a wink, with a splash and a flounce,
He must think I'm part of his watery bounce.

A feather floats by, quite lost in its flight,
It lands on my head, a comical sight.
I'm a bird with no wings, just a laugh on my face,
And it tells all the clouds to pick up the pace!

Moments like bubbles, all fizz and all cheer,
Pop goes the worries, they disappear!
I twirl in the sunshine, I slip on a shoe,
Life's a grand circus, and I'm the main crew!

So here's to each giggle and trick that we play,
To the fumbles and stumbles that brighten our day.
When time does a jiggle and memory sings,
Just dance with the moment, oh, the joy it brings!

Tides of Memory

The tides of my mind, they ebb and they flow,
Like socks that go missing, where do they go?
I search for my thoughts like a treasure map's quest,
Expecting big gold, but finding a jest.

The waves crash and giggle, they splash on the shore,
They tease me with memories, begging for more.
A seagull chuckles, as he swoops in for fries,
He caws, "Hey, buddy, stop with the sighs!"

Each moment a wave, some gentle, some wild,
I ride them with laughter, just like a child.
With a bucket of joy, and a shovel of fun,
I'm digging for treasures, oh, what a run!

So here's to remembering the giggles we stole,
Each tide brings us tales that tickle the soul.
And when the sun sets, with a wink and a grin,
I'll sail on the laughter, let the good times begin!

The River of Dreams

Down by the river where the wild ideas flow,
I fished for a thought, but caught quite a show!
A duck in a top hat asked for a dance,
I twirled and I laughed, what a curious chance!

The river whispered secrets, all frothy and bright,
"Why worry about past? Just enjoy the night!"
With bubbles that giggle and ripples that cheer,
I tossed in my worries, it turned them to sneers.

Each dream is a raft that sails on its own,
With ducks as my crew, I'm never alone!
We paddle through laughter, and drift past a cloud,
Shouting "yippee!" like we're part of a crowd.

So raise up your oars, let the good times commence,
We'll float on our whims, it makes perfect sense.
As the sun dips down, with a wink and a beam,
We'll ride on the ripples of the river of dreams!

The Ripple Effect

A pebble drops, oh what a show,
Ripples dance, to and fro.
Fish jump out, with quite a flair,
Splashing folks, unaware of where!

A dog leaps in, a soggy friend,
Chasing waves that never end.
Kids on shore, in laughter bloom,
As water splashes like a broom!

Bubbles rise, they tickle toes,
Underwater, anything goes!
A turtle peeks, with shell aglow,
Old and wise, but moves too slow.

So remember this, my merry mate,
Life's but a splash, don't hesitate!
In puddles deep or streams so wide,
Jump and giggle, enjoy the ride!

The Grace of Motion

Look at me, I float along,
Wiggling here, a dance so strong.
Watch the ducks, they glide with glee,
Quacking out, their symphony!

The wind plays tricks, it makes us sway,
Uneven paths lead us astray.
A lost shoe, what a grand surprise,
It sails away, right before our eyes!

On roller skates, I spin and twirl,
Then faceplant down, oh what a whirl!
Friends laugh loud, they can't contain,
I laugh too, through the tangled mane.

Motion's grace can take a twist,
Like trying to catch a playful mist.
Keep your balance, enjoy the spree,
In the silly ballet, we're all fancy free!

Reflections on Fluidity

A mirror pond, it makes us giggle,
As ducks dive in and do a wiggle.
Rippling faces swim with cheer,
Splashing friends, let's all be here!

Jump in quick, before it's cool,
A splashy dance, we're no one's fool!
The sun bows down, it's time to play,
As shadows stretch, they sneak away.

Puddles form, and rainbows shine,
Waves of laughter, oh how divine!
Throw your worries to the breeze,
And find your joy in silly freeze!

With every wave, there's a twisty tease,
Fluid moments, aim to please.
Take a dive, life is a treat,
In fluid laughter, feel the beat!

The Tapestry of Waves

Waves roll in, like a goofy crew,
Each one's a story, fresh and new.
A beach ball bounces, takes a flight,
Then lands on dolphin, what a sight!

Seagulls squawk, in a feathery race,
Chasing snacks, with little grace.
Umbrellas tumble like they lost a bet,
A scene so wacky, you won't forget!

With sand in toes, we build and break,
A castle falls, oh for goodness sake!
Yet laughter echoes, through sunlit days,
In every stumble, joy always stays.

So ride the waves, let giggles flow,
In this wild tapestry, let's put on a show.
With every splash, and every cheer,
Life's a beach party, let's bring in the cheer!

Tapestry of Time

A stitch here, a stitch there, we weave with glee,
Knots that slip, oh what misery!
Laughing at blunders in fabric so grand,
Who knew thread could slip from your hand?

With needles in hand, we poke and we prod,
Creating designs that sometimes are odd.
A tapestry tangled in colors so bright,
Who knew our mishaps would bring such delight?

Patterns that dance like a wild little cat,
Stitches that giggle and giggles that splat.
A masterpiece blooming, all silly and fun,
In this crazy quilt, we're never outdone!

So here's to the yarns that weave us together,
Through laughs and mistakes, whatever the weather.
A vibrant creation, a life in disarray,
We knot and we laugh; hip-hip-hooray!

Sails of Destiny

With sails unfurled, we catch the breeze,
But sometimes the wind just wants to tease.
Tacking and jibing, we sail so wide,
Oh look, we're heading where the sea cows hide!

Pirates ahead? Or just a seagull's call?
Who knew that sailing could lead to a fall?
With treasure maps drawn on the back of our hands,
We hunt for gold in the sand and the lands.

The waves keep chuckling, beneath our ship's wake,
While we sip our sodas and munch on cake.
Swabbing the deck is quite an affair,
Better watch out for that mischievous bear!

So hoist the flag, let the laughter sail,
With each little mishap, we'll tell a grand tale.
Whether we float or crash with a splash,
The fun is our bounty, and we'll always thrash!

Waves of Existence

The sea rolls in with a flip and a flop,
While we surf on moments, and sometimes just drop.
Splashing through troubles with giggles galore,
Life's a big beach party, who could ask for more?

Catching a wave, we ride with a cheer,
Until we wipe out and lose our last pier.
But laughter is buoyant; it floats us right back,
To the shores of our lives, no plans to unpack.

Seagulls above are a raucous delight,
Squawking and cawing, they join in the fight.
We barter our treasures for shells and for sand,
While waves keep crashing, as if on demand.

So here's to the splash, the tumble, the fun,
Dancing with water, under the sun.
With surfboards of dreams, we'll glide through it all,
In a world made of laughter, we'll never fall!

Threads of Tomorrow

In knitting our futures, we clumsily play,
With needles that slip in a comical way.
Purl five, knit two, and drop a few more,
Stitching our plans as we search for the door.

A scarf that's too long and a hat that won't fit,
Fashion faux pas? Yes, quite a hit!
But who cares about style when the yarn's spinning round?
With laughter on loop, joy is what's found.

In crafting our lives, we might pull a thread,
And unravel the chaos that keeps us in bed.
With coffee stains on patterns, what a crafty treat,
Life's little mishaps can't be beat!

So here's to tomorrow, with all of its flair,
We'll stitch and we'll giggle, spread happiness everywhere.
In this quilt of our making, we hold on so tight,
For tomorrow's just waiting, and laughter's in sight!

The Unseen Journey

Life's a ride on a wobbly bike,
Pedals squeaking, oh what a hike!
We dodge the puddles, drive through the rain,
With a squirrel for company, we dance in the lane.

Maps are scribbled with colors so bright,
But my GPS says we're lost tonight!
Can you take a left at the big rubber duck?
Oh dear, I think we just ran out of luck.

With snacks in the basket, we munch and we laugh,
While a goat steals our chips, what a cheeky half!
We stumble upon a parade of toy cars,
Guess this journey's written in the stars!

Under the moon, we stumble and twirl,
Life's a strange dance in a whirlpool swirl!
With giggles and tales of all that we found,
Here's to our trip, the laughter abound!

Driftwood Dreams

On shores of driftwood, we build our fate,
With castles and moats that don't quite cooperate.
Seagulls fly by, making silly swoops,
While we try to dodge their unexpected poops!

The waves crash softly, the sand holds tight,
While crabs scuttle away at a laughable sight.
Our buckets are filled with shells and with glee,
But they keep rolling back, a shell-fish spree!

A fish throws a party in an oyster shell,
And we can't stop giggling; oh, isn't it swell?
As seagull DJs drop beats from the sky,
We dance with the tide, oh my, oh my!

With sunscreen and dreams, we soak up the sun,
Yet we forgot the cooler, oh, what's to be done?
Still, laughter flows deeper than any blue sea,
In driftwood dreams, forever we're free!

Pathways of Change

Wiggly paths twist like a twisted pretzel,
As I step with confidence, oh, what a vessel!
A sign says 'Success' with an arrow that bends,
But all I can see is where the dog runs and wends.

Every corner turned holds a strange surprise,
Like bumping into a hedgehog with googly eyes.
He offers me wisdom, or maybe a snack,
In this quirky adventure, there's never a lack!

A flip-flop soldier marches without a pair,
With dreams of becoming a millionaire heir.
I'll follow his lead, for the road is absurd,
Each step filled with laughter, let's not miss a word!

The pace may be slow, but joy is our speed,
As we tumble through moments like jellybeans freed.
To be lost in the chaos is bliss on this ride,
In a world of changes, come dream by my side!

The River Within

There's a river that flows through my cluttered brain,
With ideas like fish swimming round in a train.
Some are quite silly, while others are wise,
It's a slippery path; watch for colorful pies!

My thoughts are like boats, bobbing along,
Sailing past worries, where silliness belongs.
I toss in a joke and watch it go by,
It splashes like laughter, oh me, oh my!

Sometimes it gets muddy, and I'm lost in the mess,
But a floaty unicorn makes possible stress!
It paddles beside me, all fluffy and bright,
Together we dance till we're lost to the night!

The river keeps flowing, with bubbles and cheer,
Like a confetti explosion that sweeps us near.
In the depths of my mind, where the laughter won't end,
I find that sweet magic: it's fun we can send!

www.ingramcontent.com/pod-product-compliance
Lightning Source LLC
Chambersburg PA
CBHW060141230426
43661CB00003B/520